THE FLYING ARK

WRITTEN BY
CAROLYN JACKSON

ILLUSTRATED BY
GRAHAM BARDELL

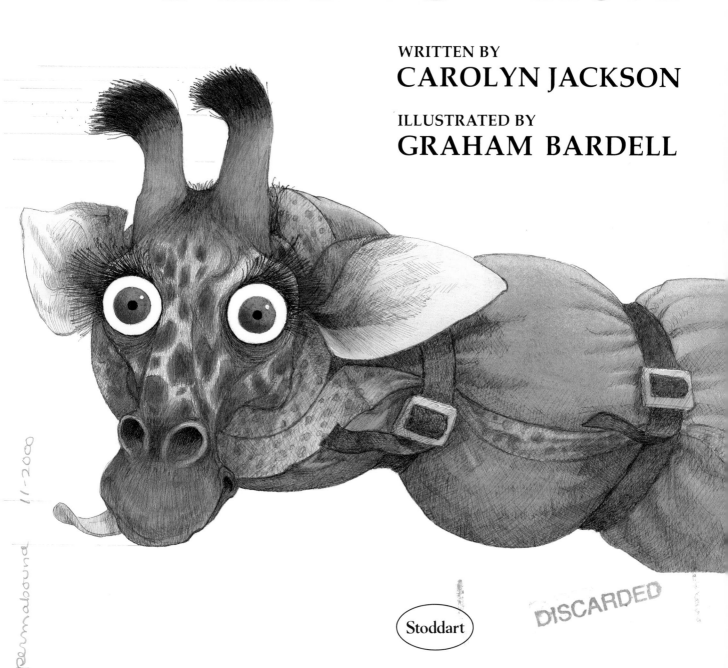

Stoddart

First published in hardcover in 1990 by
Oxford University Press Canada

First published in paperback in 1995 by
Stoddart Publishing Co. Limited
34 Lesmill Road
Toronto, Canada
M3B 2T6
(416) 445-3333

Canadian Cataloguing in Publication Data

Jackson, Carolyn, 1943–
The flying ark

ISBN 0-7737-5711-2

1. Animals, Air transportation of — Juvenile literature.
2. Animals, Air transportation of — Pictorial works.
I. Bardell, Graham.   II. Title.

HE9788.4.A55J34 1995   j387.7'44   C94-932435-3

Printed and Bound in Hong Kong

*Stoddart Publishing gratefully acknowledges the support
of the Canada Council, Ontario Ministry of Culture, Tourism and
Recreation, Ontario Arts Council, and Ontario
Publishing Centre in the development of writing and
publishing in Canada.*

For Chris, Jason, Miguela, and Lienne,
my own favourite beasties,
with a special thank you to Kathryn and Hazel.
– C.J.

For Jennifer and Tom
– G.B.

Remember the story of Noah who lived long, long ago when there was a terrible flood in the land? Noah built a huge boat called an ark. Then he invited all the animals to come aboard, two by two, so that when the flood waters dried up, the world would still have all its wonderful creatures to make it a lively and interesting place again.

That voyage on Noah's boat was probably the first trip most of the animals had ever taken, but it certainly wasn't the last. Have you ever wondered how elephants from Africa or pandas from China came to the zoo in your city? Or how the pet shop near your house got all those interesting birds and tropical fish?

Well, for many years animals had to travel by ships and trains and trucks. In those days it took a long time to cross the ocean, and some of the animals got very seasick and even fell and hurt themselves in rough weather. Bumping along in trucks or trains on long trips could be dangerous too. By the time they reached their new homes, many were sick and hurt.

But these days animals are jetsetters just like people. Often they even travel on the same planes as people! Wouldn't you be surprised if you saw a huge gorilla with a suitcase waiting in line at the ticket counter?

Of course, animals don't really check in at airports the way we do. In fact, they get very special treatment when they fly. Animal doctors and airline staff have worked hard to find ways to keep each creature happy while it travels.

You would be amazed if you could look inside the belly of a big plane carrying live animals. Each creature has its own special travelling container and each one gets exactly the right care to keep it healthy and happy.

It isn't always easy to please everyone, especially when different animals fly on the same plane. Lions and leopards, bears and bats, for instance, like to travel in the dark. They just want to rest and stay calm. But parrots and pigeons and most other birds prefer to travel in the light. If there isn't enough light to see their food, they won't eat.

Lobsters and pigs, sheep and seals like to keep very cool when they fly. But bees and tropical fish and many birds want to be warm.

Some animals need company on long trips. They feel better when they travel with their friends and relatives. But others are cranky and are happier travelling alone. You can begin to see how tricky it is to please everyone. Taking care of human passengers is easy compared to this.

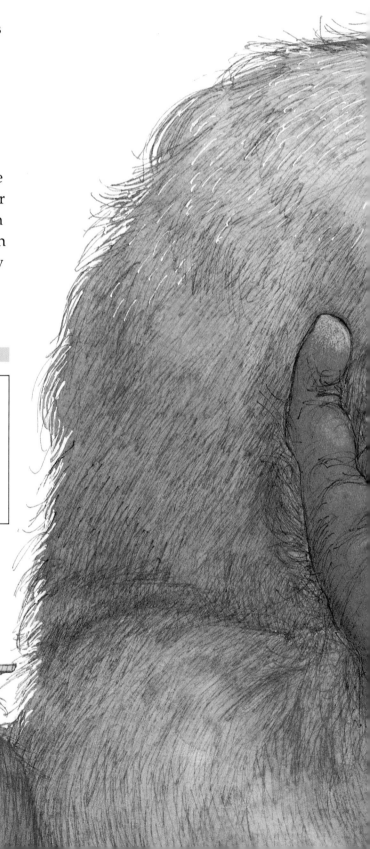

Gorillas, for instance are very nervous travellers. Even when the captain tells them to relax and enjoy the flight, they just can't seem to calm down. And when an animal as big and strong as a gorilla is upset, everybody has to watch out. Young gorillas are extremely unhappy if they are separated from their playmates, so most of the time they are allowed to stay together. But adult gorillas need cages of their own. They must be very strong, too, because gorillas just love to figure things out. They spend a lot of their time trying to get out of the container. When they are on a very long trip, gorillas snack on dainty jam and honey sandwiches and a few cookies. This special treat helps them forget their jitters and keeps them busy on the flight.

- Baby gorillas have terrible temper tantrums. Luckily they learn to be shy and peaceful when they grow up.
- Youngsters play catch and many of the same games human children do.
- Gorillas hate water. They don't swim and they hardly ever drink the stuff.

Horses are nervous too. But race horses and show horses who take part in events such as the Olympics have to travel a lot. Their own special grooms are with them, especially during takeoff and landing to make sure they don't panic. And in their specially padded stalls with canopies over their heads, most horses are able to settle down once they are in the air. Horses never have to wait in line to get on or off a plane like we do. They board just before the plane leaves and get off as soon as it lands. That way there is less time for them to get restless. And they never have to stand around and wait for their luggage. Lucky them!

- Horses were on earth 60 million years ago. At that time they were only the size of a small dog.

- Horses' hoofs are really toes. The horse is the only animal with just one toe.

- Horses can move four different ways — walking, trotting, cantering or galloping. That's pretty good for an animal, but we humans can move 20 different ways. How many can you guess?

Flamingoes travel in fashion. They wear suits on the plane. Each long-legged bird is put into a body bag made of stretchy material so that its feathers and wings won't get damaged by flapping about. Of course, the bag doesn't cover the flamingo's head. It is tied loosely around the neck. The flamingo's feet rest on soft, damp peat moss so that the webs don't dry out and crack during the trip. If flamingoes get hungry, they are given a kind of soup made of fish or minced meat and crumbled up biscuits.

- Flamingoes can't stand to be alone. They like to live in groups of 20 or more.

- Flamingoes' legs are so long that it is very hard for them to sit and then get up again. What do you think they do? They build their nests up very high, almost like stools, so they can sit and stand up again easily.

- Even in huge crowds, adult birds can pick out their own babies.

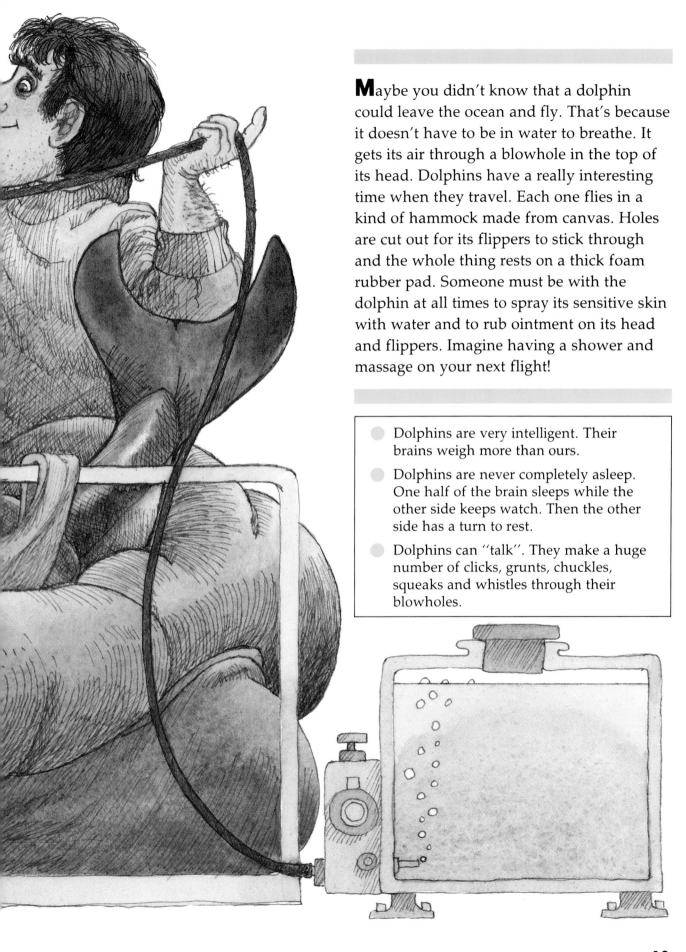

Maybe you didn't know that a dolphin could leave the ocean and fly. That's because it doesn't have to be in water to breathe. It gets its air through a blowhole in the top of its head. Dolphins have a really interesting time when they travel. Each one flies in a kind of hammock made from canvas. Holes are cut out for its flippers to stick through and the whole thing rests on a thick foam rubber pad. Someone must be with the dolphin at all times to spray its sensitive skin with water and to rub ointment on its head and flippers. Imagine having a shower and massage on your next flight!

- Dolphins are very intelligent. Their brains weigh more than ours.
- Dolphins are never completely asleep. One half of the brain sleeps while the other side keeps watch. Then the other side has a turn to rest.
- Dolphins can "talk". They make a huge number of clicks, grunts, chuckles, squeaks and whistles through their blowholes.

Ostriches don't have as much company when they fly. These strange birds travel alone in a special box made to order. It is just large enough for the ostrich to turn around in, to lie in and to stand up in. There is no room for exercise because the big birds might hurt themselves if they had enough room to jog around. Besides, their legs are big and powerful enough to bend metal when they kick. Ostriches are much better off if they are left to eat their juicy carrot and apple snacks in peace. Airline workers must be careful to make sure there is nothing shiny left too close to the cage, though. These birds have a weird appetite for stones and anything glittery that catches their eye — even watches and pocketknives. The stones help them digest their food. But telling the time would be difficult if you carried your watch in your stomach, wouldn't it?

- Ostriches are the world's largest birds and they are the only ones who can roar.
- Ostrich eggs are good to eat, but they are so big that it would take about four hours to hardboil one. In Africa, the shells are sometimes used as food bowls.
- Ostriches can drink salty water as well as fresh because they have special glands in their noses that get rid of salt.

Kangaroos have special containers too. They tend to get just a bit jumpy in a plane. You can guess what that means. A big headache! So their travelling boxes have thick padding on the ceilings. That way, kangaroos arrive feeling bouncy, but without lumpy heads.

By now you can begin to see why each animal needs special attention. And you can understand why they all need boxes or stalls. Can you imagine what it would be like to be in a plane full of jittery gorillas, jogging ostriches and jumpy kangaroos? That would be enough to make everyone twitchy.

- At birth, kangaroos are so small that several could fit into a teaspoon.
- Kangaroos know where to dig to find water underground. They can go for weeks without water as long as they have grass and leaves to eat. Kangaroos are excellent swimmers.
- When they are hot, kangaroos lick their armpits to cool down.

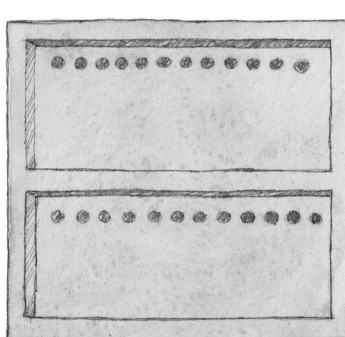

Nobody is quite sure what an octopus thinks when it travels. It sits inside a thick, strong plastic bag. The bag is less than half-filled with water and then oxygen is pumped in through the top before it is sealed. If the trip is very long and the plane stops along the way, zoo keepers come out to the airport. They give the octopus more oxygen so it can continue its journey without feeling faint.

- The shy octopus changes colour depending on its mood. When it is angry, the octopus turns red. When it is frightened, it turns white. And when it just wants to hide, it turns blue or green to blend in with the ocean.

- If an octopus loses an arm, it just grows a new one.

- When an octopus arm touches something, it tastes and smells the object as well as feeling it.

- Scientists know that octopuses can plan and remember things. They have even been taught to recognize letters!

Believe it or not, bees like to travel in big crowds inside a fat, round tube. The tubes have pieces of mesh inside for the bees to cling to. Of course, the queen bee has her own royal seat inside a tiny box fastened to the mesh. The rest of the bees cluster around her and eat a kind of sugary jelly from a feeding tube. The ends of the big container are fastened tightly so that none of the busy buzzers can fly around the plane.

- Bees are the gold medal winners in the weightlifting department. They can lift or pull something that is 300 times heavier than they are.
- Bees have five eyes — three on top of the head and one on each side.
- Bees are deaf. Too bad, but at least they don't have to listen to all that bothersome buzzing.

Fortunately for all concerned, elephants have steady nerves when they travel. But they do have a rather embarrassing problem. They must drink a lot, you see, just before they board the plane in their huge crates. Elephants need about 100 litres of water every day. That's the same as drinking 100 cartons of milk. It's easy to guess what happens a little later. When they have to go, they really have to go! Obviously, elephants are just a little large for airline washrooms. So, their crates are filled knee high with peat moss and wood shavings just to soak up the problem.

- Elephants are the largest land animals.
- Elephants are the only animals with four knees, yet they are the only ones who can't jump.
- Elephants purr like cats when they are eating peacefully.
- Elephants have huge teeth, but they only have a couple at a time. When they are worn down from too much chomping, new ones pop up. After 24 teeth have been used, an elephant must eat soft food because no more teeth will grow.
- An elephant's trunk is really its nose and upper lip joined together. The trunk has 40,000 muscles! It is strong enough to rip up trees, yet delicate enough to pick up a tiny sugar cube.

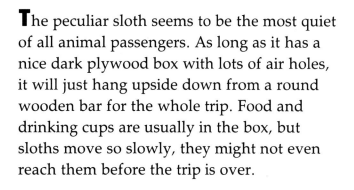

The peculiar sloth seems to be the most quiet of all animal passengers. As long as it has a nice dark plywood box with lots of air holes, it will just hang upside down from a round wooden bar for the whole trip. Food and drinking cups are usually in the box, but sloths move so slowly, they might not even reach them before the trip is over.

- Sloths eat, sleep and have their babies upside down. They move so slowly that some of them spend their whole lives in just one tree.
- The sloth's hair grows from its stomach round to its back. This way, when it rains, the water follows the way the hair grows and runs right off. No soggy tummy puddles.
- Sloth stomachs are a bilious green colour because plants, called algae, grow in the grooves in the sloth's hair. This helps sloths hide from their enemies because they just look like more green leaves in a tree.

Hummingbirds are just the opposite. They move so fast you can hardly see them. Twelve or so usually travel together in the same wooden and mesh box. The box has curtains too, so that the birds can have some privacy but still get enough light to find their feeding bottles. They drink lots of nectar and water. The rest of the time they sit on their perches. They are probably glad to take a break from flying themselves.

- Tiny ruby-throated hummingbirds hardly need a plane to travel. Every year, on their way from Canada to South America, they fly over the water of the huge Gulf of Mexico without stopping.

- Hummingbirds beat their wings faster than any other bird — 90 times in just one second. To do that much work they have to eat almost all day long.

- Because they hardly ever use them, a hummingbird's feet have become very weak. They are good for perching, but not for hopping or walking.

- Hummingbirds use delicate spiderweb strands to tie their tiny nests together.

Penguins insist on keeping their cool on a trip. If the temperature becomes too warm in the plane, or at any of the stops along the way, penguins get puffy feet, which is not at all attractive or comfortable. Their heads start to droop, too. That gives them a very peculiar and sad appearance. They can be fixed up in a jiffy, though, by having a cold shower. And a fresh fish or two always helps.

- Adelie penguins return to the same place every year to hatch their eggs. They travel a great distance and find their way by watching the position of the sun and stars.

- A boy Adelie penguin wins his own special girlfriend by offering her an especially nice stone. If she accepts it with a little bow, he knows she will be his Valentine.

- Emperor penguins usually walk with a funny waddle, but when they are in a hurry, they lie down on their stomachs and toboggan over the ice and snow. They use their flippers to make themselves go faster.

- Only the father Emperors hatch the eggs. They hold them on top of their feet for two months and cover them with a special pouch to keep them warm — even when it is 50 below.

One of the most difficult of all animals to fit in a plane is the giraffe. For one thing, the shy, gentle creature is so nervous that it can get quite frightened when it has to be moved. And of course its neck is so long that special padding is needed to protect it. For some strange reason, giraffes prefer to travel backwards, with their heads facing the tail of the airplane. Maybe they just don't want to face going to a new place.

- The giraffe is the tallest animal. Some of them grow to be as high as a two-storey building.
- Even though a giraffe's neck is so long, it has just seven neck bones — exactly the same as people.
- Giraffes do lie down to sleep. They lay their long necks along their backs to rest. But they only snooze for about six minutes at a time. That's hardly enough time for sweet dreams.

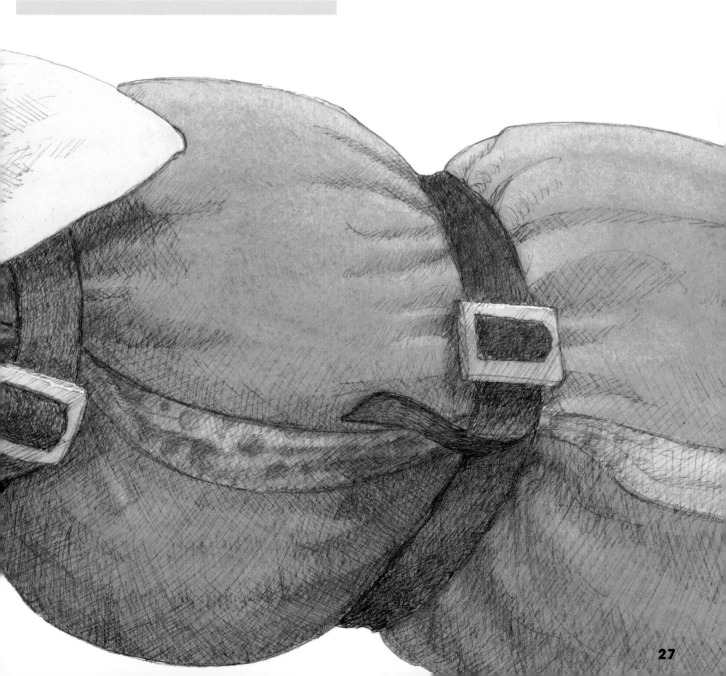

Camels, on the other hand, aren't shy at all. But they can be downright nasty sometimes. Just in case their tempers get too hot, camels all wear muzzles while they travel. They make the trip in stalls, like horses, but they always look like they'd rather be somewhere else. The other animal passengers just try to ignore the bad-tempered beasts. What else can you do? There's one in every crowd.

- Camels are born without any humps at all. The humps appear as they grow older.

- Because of the fat and moisture it stores in its humps, a camel really can go for days without water, even in the hot desert.

- A camel has a groove that runs from each nostril to the split in its lip. That way, anything dripping from its nose can be caught in its mouth. Disgusting, but a good way to save moisture.

Sometimes when very special animals travel, they are given star treatment. There aren't many pandas left in the world, so when one or two of them leave China to visit a zoo somewhere else, they are treated like royalty. The airlines take out some of the seats in the first class passenger section so that the big black and white creatures can sit in their cages right up in front. Zookeepers and officials from China sit near the cages to make sure curious passengers don't get too close to the pampered pandas.

- Pandas live a secret life in the bamboo forests of China. They like being alone, so nobody knows very much about them.

- Pandas spend almost 12 hours a day eating their favourite food — bamboo trees. The bones in their wrists have developed into thumbs, like ours, to help them hold the bamboo.

- When they are born, pandas are smaller than human babies and they are completely white.

- Scientists think that the panda is actually a kind of giant raccoon, and not a bear at all.

Of course, not all the animals are lucky enough to travel in the first class section, but every single one of them gets its own special treatment along the way. Everyone works very hard to make sure that all the world can share the fascinating and beautiful animals living in it. Now wouldn't Noah be pleased?